Vishnu Chalisa

Vishnu Chalisa

Published in Sanskriti Press
Rupa Publications India Pvt. Ltd 2025
161-B/4, Gulmohar House,
Yusuf Sarai Community Centre,
New Delhi 110049

Sales centres:
Bengaluru Chennai
Hyderabad Kolkata Mumbai

P-ISBN: 978-93-7003-107-4
E-ISBN: 978-93-7003-723-6

First impression 2025

10 9 8 7 6 5 4 3 2 1

Printed in India

Contents

Introduction

The Vishnu Chalisa is a sacred forty-verse hymn composed in Awadhi-Hindi poetic meter. It venerates Lord Vishnu, the eternal preserver in the Hindu Trimurti. Revered by millions across generations, this Chalisa encapsulates the essence of Vaishnavism. This devotional tradition sees Vishnu as the Supreme God (Parabrahman) and the compassionate guardian of cosmic order (*Rta*).

Rooted in Bhakti Yoga, the Vishnu Chalisa is not merely a song of praise; it is a spiritual practice that combines mantra, kirtan, and scriptural wisdom into a simple yet profound poetic composition accessible to all. Though the exact authorship is uncertain, it follows the revered Chalisa tradition popularized in North India by saint-poets such as Tulsidas, who composed the Hanuman Chalisa. These Chalisas serve as devotional distillations of vast spiritual philosophies.

In the Vishnu Chalisa, Lord Vishnu is praised as Jagatpati (Lord of the Universe), Hari (remover of sins), and Antaryami (inner controller). Each verse illustrates his divine virtues: his infinite mercy, supreme knowledge, eternal form, and his role as Yogeshwar (master of yogis). It recounts his ten principal avatars (Dashavatara)—divine incarnations through which he descends to protect dharma and annihilate evil. These stories are not just mythological events but metaphysical symbols of the soul's struggle and salvation.

Chanting or listening to the Vishnu Chalisa with faith is believed to purify the heart, strengthen mental clarity, dissolve negative karmas, and invoke divine blessings for both material and spiritual progress. Traditionally recited on Thursdays, Ekadashi, and Vishnu-centric festivals like Vaikuntha Ekadashi or Diwali, it forms a vital part of household rituals and temple worship.

In essence, the Vishnu Chalisa is a divine bridge between the devotee and the Supreme Being—inviting the Lord into one's heart with humility, love, and surrender.

Chalīsa

।। दोहा ।।

विष्णु सुनिए विनय सेवक की चितलाय ।
कीरत कुछ वर्णन करूं दीजै ज्ञान बताय ।।

Vishnu suniye vinay
sevak ki chitalay
Keerat kuch varnan
karoon deeje gyaan batay

O Vishnu, please listen to your servant's humble prayer.
Grant me the wisdom to describe a bit of your divine glory.

॥ चौपाई ॥

नमो विष्णु भगवान खरारी,
कष्ट नशावन अखिल बिहारी।
प्रबल जगत में शक्ति तुम्हारी,
त्रिभुवन फैल रही उजियारी ॥

Namo Vishnu Bhagwan kharari,
kasht nashaavan akhil bihaari.
Prabal jagat mein shakti tumhaari,
tribhuvan phail rahi ujiyaari.

Salutations to Lord Vishnu, destroyer of
evil and remover of all pain.
Your immense power spreads divine light
across all three worlds.

सुन्दर रूप मनोहर सूरत,
सरल स्वभाव मोहनी मूरत।
तन पर पीताम्बर अति सोहत,
बैजन्ती माला मन मोहत ।।

Sundar roop manohar surat, saral swabhaav mohini moorat.
Tan par peetambar ati sohat,
Baijanti mala man mohat.

Your beautiful and enchanting form is sweet and serene.
You wear a shining yellow robe and a Vaijayanti garland that captivates the heart.

शंख चक्र कर गदा बिराजे,
देखत दैत्य असुर दल भाजे।
सत्य धर्म मद लोभ न गाजे,
काम क्रोध मद लोभ न छाजे ।।

Shankh chakra kar gada biraaje,
dekhat daitya asur dal bhaaje.
Satya dharm mad lobh na gaaje,
kaam krodh mad lobh na chaaje.

With conch, discus, and mace in hand,
demons flee at your sight.
You are untouched by pride, lust, greed,
or anger—ever rooted in truth and
dharma.

सन्तभक्त सज्जन मनरंजन,
दनुज असुर दुष्टन दल गंजन।
सुख उपजाय कष्ट सब भंजन,
दोष मिटाय करत जन सज्जन ॥

Sant bhakt sajjan man ranjan,
danuj asur dushtan dal ganjan.
Sukh upjaay kasht sab bhanjan,
dosh mitay karat jan sajjan.

You bring joy to saints and devotees,
destroyer of demon hordes.
You create happiness, end all pain, and
remove sins from the good-hearted.

पाप काट भव सिन्धु उतारण,
कष्ट नाशकर भक्त उबारण।
करत अनेक रूप प्रभु धारण,
केवल आप भक्ति के कारण ।।

Paap kaat bhav sindhu utaaran,
kasht naashkar bhakt ubaaran.
Karat anek roop prabhu dhaaran,
keval aap bhakti ke kaaran.

You destroy sins and ferry souls across the ocean of existence.
Taking many forms, you save your devotees purely out of love.

धरणि धेनु बन तुम्हिं पुकारा,
तब तुम रूप राम का धारा।
भार उतार असुर दल मारा,
रावण आदिक को संहारा ।।

Dharani dhenu ban tumhi pukaara,
tab tum roop Ram ka dhaara.
Bhaar utaar asur dal maara,
Ravan aadik ko sanhaara.

When Earth cried out as a cow, you appeared as Shri Ram.
You destroyed the burden of demons like Ravan to restore peace.

आप वाराह रूप बनाया,
हरण्याक्ष को मार गिराया।
धर मत्स्य तन सिन्धु बनाया,
चौदह रतनन को निकलाया ।।

Aap Varaah roop banaya,
Harnyaaksh ko maar giraya.
Dhar Matsya tan sindhu banaya,
chaudah ratnan ko nikalaya.

You took the form of a boar to kill
Hiranyaksha.
As a fish, you retrieved the fourteen
treasures from the ocean.

अमिलख असुरन द्वन्द मचाया,
रूप मोहनी आप दिखाया।
देवन को अमृत पान कराया,
असुरन को छवि से बहलाया ।।

Amilakh asuran dvand machaya,
roop Mohini aap dikhaya.
Devan ko amrit paan karaya,
asuran ko chhavi se bahlaya.

In the fight for nectar, you appeared as Mohini.
You gave nectar to the gods, and enchanted demons with your beauty.

कूर्म रूप धर सिन्धु मझाया,
मन्द्राचल गिरि तुरत उठाया।
शंकर का तुम फन्द छुड़ाया,
भस्मासुर को रूप दिखाया ॥

Kurm roop dhar sindhu majhaya,
Mandrachal giri turat uthaya.
Shankar ka tum phand chhudaaya,
Bhasmasur ko roop dikhaya.

You took the form of a tortoise to support the mountain during ocean-churning. You rescued Shiva and outwitted Bhasmasur with your divine disguise.

वेदन को जब असुर डुबाया,
कर प्रबन्ध उन्हें ढुंढवाया।
मोहित बनकर खलहि नचाया,
उसही कर से भस्म कराया ॥

Vedan ko jab asur dubaaya,
kar prabandh unhein dhundhvaaya.
Mohit bankar khalahi nachaaya,
usi kar se bhasm karaya.

When demons hid the Vedas, you arranged for their recovery.
You enchanted the wicked and caused them to self-destruct.

असुर जलन्धर अति बलदाई,
शंकर से उन कीन्ह लड़ाई।
हार पार शिव सकल बनाई,
कीन सती से छल खल जाई ॥

Asur Jalandhar ati baldai,
Shankar se un keen ladaai.
Haar paar Shiv sakal banaai,
keen Sati se chhal khal jaai.

The powerful demon Jalandhar fought with Shiva.
He tricked Sati to gain power over Shiva.

सुमिरन कीन तुम्हें शिवरानी,
बतलाई सब विपत कहानी।
तब तुम बने मुनीश्वर ज्ञानी,
वृन्दा की सब सुरति भुलानी ॥

Sumiran keen tumhe Shivraani,
batlaayi sab vipat kahaani.
Tab tum bane Munishwar gyaani,
Vrinda ki sab surati bhulaani.

Shiva's consort meditated upon you and told you the tale.
You then appeared as a sage and caused Vrinda to forget her vow.

देखत तीन दनुज शैतानी,
वृन्दा आय तुम्हें लपटानी।
हो स्पर्श धर्म क्षति मानी,
हना असुर उर शिव शैतानी ।।

Dekhat teen danuj shaitaani,
Vrinda aay tumhe lapatani.
Ho sparsh dharm kshati maani,
hana asur ur Shiv shaitaani.

Seeing the vile demon, Vrinda embraced you, unaware.
Her vow was broken, and Shiva destroyed the demon in wrath.

तुमने ध्रुव प्रह्लाद उबारे,
हिरणाकुश आदिक खल मारे।
गणिका और अजामिल तारे,
बहुत भक्त भव सिन्धु उतारे ॥

Tumne Dhruv Prahlaad ubaare,
Hiranyakush aadik khal maare.
Ganika aur Ajamila taare,
bahut bhakt bhav sindhu utaare.

You protected Dhruv and Prahlad, and destroyed demons like Hiranyakush. You saved the courtesan and Ajamila, ferrying many devotees across the ocean of life.

हरहु सकल संताप हमारे,
कृपा करहु हरि सिरजन हारे।
देखहुं मैं निज दरश तुम्हारे,
दीन बन्धु भक्तन हितकारे ।।

Harahu sakal santaap hamaare,
kripa karahu Hari sirjan haare.
Dekhun main nij darash tumhaare,
deen bandhu bhaktan hitkaare.

Remove all my sufferings, O Creator Hari,
show your mercy.
Let me behold your divine form, O friend
of the meek and protector of devotees.

चहत आपका सेवक दर्शन,
करहु दया अपनी मधुसूदन।
जानूं नहीं योग्य जब पूजन,
होय यज्ञ स्तुति अनुमोदन ॥

Chahat aapka sevak darshan,
karahu daya apni Madhusudan.
Janoon nahin yogya jab poojan,
hoy yajna stuti anumodan.

Your servant longs for your vision, O
Madhusudan, show your grace.
Though I don't know proper worship, may
this praise be accepted as sacrifice.

शीलदया सन्तोष सुलक्षण,
विदित नहीं व्रतबोध विलक्षण।
करहुं आपका किस विधि पूजन,
कुमति विलोक होत दुख भीषण ॥

Sheel daya santosh sulakshan,
vidit nahin vratabodh vilakshan.
Karoon aapka kis vidhi poojan,
kumati vilok hot dukh bhishan.

Virtue, compassion, and vows—I lack
knowledge of these traits.
How should I worship you, when
ignorance brings me such sorrow?

करहुं प्रणाम कौन विधि सुमिरण,
कौन भांति मैं करहु समर्पण।
सुर मुनि करत सदा सेवकाई,
हर्षित रहत परम गति पाई ।।

Karoon pranam kaun vidhi sumiran,
kaun bhaanti main karoon samarpan.
Sur muni karat sada sevakai,
harshit rahat param gati paai.

What way should I bow, or remember, or
offer myself to you?
Even gods and sages serve you always,
rejoicing in the supreme state.

दीन दुखिन पर सदा सहाई,
निज जन जान लेव अपनाई।
पाप दोष संताप नशाओ,
भव बन्धन से मुक्त कराओ ।।

Deen dukhin par sada sahaai,
nij jan jaan lev apnaai.
Paap dosh santaap nashaao,
bhav bandhan se mukt karaao.

You ever help the poor and sorrowful, accepting them as your own.
Destroy their sins and afflictions, and free them from worldly bondage.

सुत सम्पति दे सुख उपजाओ,
निज चरणन का दास बनाओ।
निगम सदा ये विनय सुनावै,
पढ़ै सुनै सो जन सुख पावै ॥

Sut sampati de sukh upjaao,
nij charanan ka daas banao.
Nigam sada ye vinay sunaavai,
padhai sunai so jan sukh paavai.

Grant children and wealth, bring happiness, and make me your humble servant.
The scriptures repeat this prayer—whoever reads or hears it is blessed with peace.

॥ दोहा ॥

भक्त हृदय में वास करें पूर्ण कीजिये काज ।
शंख चक्र और गदा पद्म हे विष्णु महाराज ॥

Bhakt hriday mein vaas
karein poorn keejiyai kaaj
Shankh chakra aur gada padm
he Vishnu Maharaj

O Lord Vishnu, reside in the hearts of your devotees and fulfill their righteous tasks.
Wielder of conch, discus, mace, and lotus—O King Vishnu, bless us always.

विष्णु आरती

ॐ जय जगदीश हरे, स्वामी! जय जगदीश हरे।
भक्त जनों के संकट, क्षण में दूर करे ॥

ॐ जय जगदीश हरे।

जो ध्यावे फल पावे, दुःख विनसे मन का।
स्वामी दुःख विनसे मन का।
सुख सम्पत्ति घर आवे, कष्ट मिटे तन का ॥

ॐ जय जगदीश हरे।

मात-पिता तुम मेरे, शरण गहूँ मैं किसकी।
स्वामी शरण गहूँ मैं किसकी।
तुम बिन और न दूजा, आस करूँ जिसकी ॥

ॐ जय जगदीश हरे।

तुम पूरण परमात्मा, तुम अन्तर्यामी।
स्वामी तुम अन्तर्यामी।
पारब्रह्म परमेश्वर, तुम सबके स्वामी ॥

ॐ जय जगदीश हरे।

तुम करुणा के सागर, तुम पालन-कर्ता।
स्वामी तुम पालन-कर्ता।
मैं मूरख खल कामी, कृपा करो भर्ता ॥

ॐ जय जगदीश हरे।

तुम हो एक अगोचर, सबके प्राणपति।
स्वामी सबके प्राणपति।
किस विधि मिलूँ दयामय,
तुमको मैं कुमति ॥

ॐ जय जगदीश हरे।

दीनबन्धु दुखहर्ता, तुम ठाकुर मेरे।
स्वामी तुम ठाकुर मेरे।
अपने हाथ उठाओ, द्वार पड़ा तेरे ॥

ॐ जय जगदीश हरे।

विषय-विकार मिटाओ, पाप हरो देवा।
स्वमी पाप हरो देवा।
श्रद्धा-भक्ति बढ़ाओ, सन्तन की सेवा ॥

ॐ जय जगदीश हरे।

श्री जगदीशजी की आरती, जो कोई नर गावे।
स्वामी जो कोई नर गावे।
कहत शिवानन्द स्वामी, सुख संपत्ति पावे ॥

ॐ जय जगदीश हरे।

Vishnu Aarti

Om Jai Jagdish Hare,
Swami! Jai Jagdish Hare
Bhakt jano ke sankat,
kshan mein door kare
Om Jai Jagdish Hare

Jo dhyave phal pave,
dukh vinse man ka
Swami dukh vinse man ka
Sukh sampatti ghar aave,
kasht mite tan ka
Om Jai Jagdish Hare

Maat-pita tum mere,
sharan gahoo main kiski
Swami sharan gahoo main kiski
Tum bin aur na dooja,
aas karoon jiski
Om Jai Jagdish Hare

Tum pooran parmatma,
tum antaryaami
Swami tum antaryaami
Parabrahma Parmeshwar,
tum sabke Swami
Om Jai Jagdish Hare

Tum karuna ke saagar,
tum paalan-karta
Swami tum paalan-karta
Main moorakh khal kaami,
kripa karo bharta
Om Jai Jagdish Hare

Tum ho ek agochar,
sabke praanpati
Swami sabke praanpati
Kis vidhi miloon dayamay,
tumko main kumati
Om Jai Jagdish Hare

Deenabandhu dukh-harta,
tum Thakur mere
Swami tum Thakur mere
Apne haath uthao, dwaar pada tere
Om Jai Jagdish Hare

Vishay-vikaar mitaao,
paap haro Deva
Swami paap haro Deva
Shraddha-bhakti badhaao,
santan ki seva
Om Jai Jagdish Hare

Shri Jagdishji ki Aarti,
jo koi nar gaave
Swami jo koi nar gaave
Kahat Shivanand Swami,
sukh sampatti paave
Om Jai Jagdish Hare

Vishnu Aarti

Om, Victory to Lord of the
Universe, O Lord! Victory to
You, Lord of the Universe
You remove the troubles
of your devotees instantly.
Om, Victory to Lord
of the Universe

Whoever meditates
on you receives
your blessings,
and the sorrow

of the mind is destroyed.
O Lord, the sorrow of
the mind is destroyed.
Happiness and wealth
enter the home, and bodily
suffering disappears.
Om, Victory to Lord of the
Universe

You are my mother and
father—whom else can
I take refuge in?
O Lord, whom else can
I take refuge in?
There is no one else besides
you, from whom

I can hope for support.
Om, Victory to Lord
of the Universe

You are the complete Supreme
Soul, the inner dweller
of all beings.
O Lord, you are the
inner dweller.
The Supreme Brahman, the
Highest God—you are the
Lord of all.
Om, Victory to Lord
of the Universe

You are the ocean of
compassion, the nurturer
and protector.
O Lord, you are the nurturer.
I am ignorant, sinful, and full
of desires—please show mercy,
O Lord.
Om, Victory to Lord
of the Universe

You are the indescribable one,
the Lord of all living beings.
O Lord, you are the
master of all lives.
How can I, with my impure

mind, approach you,
O Merciful One?
Om, Victory to Lord
of the Universe

Friend of the helpless,
remover of suffering,
you are my Master.
O Lord, you are my Master.
Lift your hand in blessing—
I lie at your doorstep.
Om, Victory to Lord
of the Universe

Remove worldly desires
and sins, O Divine One.

O Lord, remove all sins.
Increase my devotion and
faith, and let me serve
the saints.
Om, Victory to Lord
of the Universe

Whoever sings the aarti of
Lord Jagdish with devotion,
O Lord, whoever sings
with devotion,
Says Swami Shivananda—
they will gain happiness and
prosperity.
Om, Victory to Lord
of the Universe